IT CONTRACTING UNLOCKED

The Essential Guide to Building a Successful Career in IT Contracting in the UK

Ravi Matharu

Copyright Notice

© 2024 Ravi Matharu. All rights reserved.

No part of this book may be reproduced, stored in a retrieval system, or transmitted in any form or by any means—electronic, mechanical, photocopying, recording, or otherwise—without the prior written permission of the author, except in the case of brief quotations embodied in critical articles and reviews. Unauthorised reproduction or distribution of this material is prohibited by law and may result in severe civil and criminal penalties.

The moral rights of the author have been asserted.

Published in the United Kingdom.

ISBN: 9798346643647

Any trademarks, service marks, product names, or named features are assumed to be the property of their respective owners and are used for reference only. There is no implied endorsement if they are mentioned.

Disclaimer

The information provided in *IT Contracting Unlocked* is intended for general informational and educational purposes only. While every effort has been made to ensure the accuracy of the information contained in this book, it should not be construed as legal, financial, or professional advice. Tax laws, regulations, and best practices are subject to change, and the specific circumstances of your contracting business may vary.

Readers are encouraged to seek professional advice from a qualified accountant, tax advisor, or solicitor regarding their specific financial, tax, and legal situations. The author and publisher make no representations or warranties with respect to the completeness, accuracy, or applicability of the contents of this book and disclaim any liability arising directly or indirectly from the use or reliance on the information provided.

The reader acknowledges that the use of this book is solely at their own risk and that neither the author nor the publisher shall be held liable for any direct, indirect, incidental, or consequential damages arising from the use of the information herein.

This book does not establish any kind of client relationship between the author and the reader. It is always advisable to consult with professionals for individual advice tailored to your needs.

For Karishma and Kaira,

who fill my heart with joy every day.

Contents

Introduction 9

Chapter 1 Getting Started with IT Contracting in the UK 11

Chapter 2 Choosing Your Business Structure 21

Chapter 3 The Contracting Market in the UK 33

Chapter 4 IR35 Legislation and Tax Implications 43

Chapter 5 Taxes, Accounting, and Financial Management for Contractors
.... 51

Chapter 6 Managing Contracts and Clients 65

Chapter 7 Working with Agencies 79

Chapter 8 Essential Tools and Techniques for IT Contractors 93

Chapter 9 Contracting from Outside the UK 107

Chapter 10 Preparing for the Future of IT Contracting 121

Conclusion 133

Final Thoughts 139

Appendices 141

About The Author 153

Introduction

Welcome to *IT Contracting Unlocked*, your essential guide to navigating the UK's dynamic and rewarding world of IT contracting. Whether you're new to the industry or an experienced contractor looking to stay current with the latest legislation, this book is designed to equip you with the knowledge, tools, and techniques needed to succeed. The UK is a hotbed of technological innovation and opportunity, with companies constantly seeking specialised skills to drive digital transformation and growth. This demand has made IT contracting a popular career path, offering flexibility, attractive earnings, and the chance to work on cutting-edge projects.

However, with these benefits come complexities. From setting up a business structure and choosing between umbrella companies and limited companies to navigating IR35 regulations and managing your finances, contracting requires knowledge and preparation. This book aims to demystify the process and provide practical advice tailored to the UK market, including upcoming tax changes and considerations for those contracting from outside the UK. Each chapter includes checklists, case studies, and tools to help you make informed decisions at every stage of your contracting journey. Let this guide be your trusted companion as you explore, establish, and excel in the world of IT contracting.

Chapter 1

Getting Started with IT Contracting in the UK

The journey to becoming a successful IT contractor in the UK begins with understanding the unique structure, benefits, and challenges of contracting and setting up your business appropriately. This chapter will walk you through the basics of IT contracting in the UK, from evaluating the pros and cons to registering your business and obtaining the necessary skills.

1.1 Understanding IT Contracting vs. Permanent Employment

Before entering contracting, it's essential to understand how it differs from traditional employment and weigh the benefits and challenges.

What is IT Contracting?

IT contracting involves working independently on short- to medium-term projects for various clients. Contractors are typically hired for their specialised skills and may move from one project to another based-on demand. Unlike permanent employment, where individuals receive a fixed salary and benefits, contractors earn based on the duration or scope of each contract. They must handle their own taxes, insurance, and other business-related expenses.

Advantages and Challenges of Contracting

- **Advantages**:
    - **Higher Income Potential**: Contractors often earn more per hour or day than full-time employees, as they're hired for specialised, high-demand skills.
    - **Flexibility**: Contractors can select projects based on interest, availability, and career goals, often with more control over their work schedule.
    - **Skill Development**: Exposure to different industries and projects accelerates skill development, making contractors highly adaptable and experienced.

- **Challenges**:
    - **Irregular Income**: Contracts may vary in length, and there could be gaps between projects, requiring financial planning.
    - **Administrative Burden**: Contractors must handle their own taxes, accounting, and legal requirements, which can be time-consuming.
    - **Less Job Security**: Contracts are time-bound, meaning job security depends on securing new projects regularly.

Decision-Making Checklist

Use the following checklist to assess if contracting is the right fit for you:

- Are you comfortable with financial fluctuations?
- Do you value flexibility over stability?
- Are you prepared to manage administrative tasks and tax obligations?
- Do you have marketable skills that are in high demand?
- Are you motivated to seek new projects and clients regularly?

1.2 Setting Up as an IT Contractor in the UK

Setting up your contracting business requires selecting the right business structure, registering with the appropriate authorities, and establishing essential business accounts.

Choosing Between Business Structures

New contractors typically choose between working through an umbrella company or setting up their own limited company, though sole trader status is also an option.

1. Limited Company vs. Umbrella Company

A limited company gives contractors full control over financial and tax matters but requires more administration. On the other hand, Umbrella companies simplify payroll and tax deductions by handling them on your behalf, though this comes with service fees.

Comparison Table:

Limited Company	Umbrella Company
Full control over finances and expenses	Simplified, with payroll handled by the umbrella company
More tax-efficient with salary and dividends	No dividend options; taxed through PAYE
Legal responsibilities as a company director	No company director responsibilities
Suitable for long-term contracting	Better for short-term or IR35-inside roles

2. Registering as a Limited Company

To establish a limited company in the UK, follow these steps:

1. **Register with Companies House**: Submit your company name and address and appoint at least one director and shareholder.

2. **Obtain a Unique Taxpayer Reference (UTR)**: HMRC will issue a UTR for corporation tax purposes after registration.

3. **Open a Business Bank Account**: Set up a dedicated business account to separate personal and business finances.

4. **Hire an Accountant**: An accountant can help with compliance, financial planning, and tax filing, which can save time and prevent costly mistakes.

3. Setting Up Through an Umbrella Company

If you choose an umbrella company, the setup is simpler. You become an employee of the umbrella company employee, and they manage your payroll, tax deductions, and insurance. This option is ideal for shorter contracts or for contractors who prefer minimal administration.

4. Registering as a Sole Trader

For contractors who choose the sole trader route, the registration process is simple:

- Register with HMRC for self-assessment.
- Keep accurate records of income and expenses.
- Note that as a sole trader, you are personally liable for any business debts.

1.3 Essential Skills and Certifications for IT Contractors

To remain competitive, contractors need to possess in-demand technical skills and certifications, as well as important soft skills for managing clients and projects.

Technical Skills in Demand

In the UK, high-demand skills include:

- **Cybersecurity**: Certified professionals with qualifications like CISSP, CISM, or CompTIA Security+.
- **Cloud Computing**: Skills in platforms like AWS, Azure, or Google Cloud are sought after for cloud migration and management projects.
- **Data Science and Analytics**: Data professionals skilled in Python, R, or SQL and familiar with tools like Tableau or Power BI.
- **Software Development**: Full-stack and specialised developers in JavaScript, Python, Java, and modern frameworks.

Certifications and Soft Skills

Certifications can strengthen your credibility and open doors to high-paying contracts. Examples include:

- **AWS Certified Solutions Architect, Microsoft Certified: Azure Solutions Architect Expert, Certified Information Systems Security Professional (CISSP)**.
- **Project Management**: For contractors who take on leadership roles, project management certifications (e.g., PMP, ScrumMaster) are valuable.

Essential Soft Skills

- **Client Communication**: Building and maintaining client relationships relies on effective and clear communication.

- **Adaptability**: Contractors who can adapt quickly to new environments and technologies have an advantage.

- **Time Management**: Effective scheduling and priority-setting allow contractors to meet deadlines and balance multiple projects if necessary.

1.4 Setup Process Flowchart

Below is a flowchart outlining the process for getting started as an IT contractor in the UK.

Decide on Business Structure	Limited Company - Requires registration with Companies House, UTR, bank account, accountant
	Umbrella Company - Choose umbrella provider, sign up, payroll managed by umbrella
	Sole Trader - Register with HMRC for self-assessment, personal liability
Obtain Necessary Skills and Certifications	Research in-demand skills for IT (e.g., Cybersecurity, Cloud Computing)
	Obtain relevant certifications (AWS, PMP, CISSP, etc.)
Open a Business Bank Account	Separate personal and business finances to streamline accounting
Hire an Accountant (recommended for a Limited Company)	Assists with tax, payroll, and compliance requirements
Register for VAT (if required or advantageous)	Determine eligibility (VAT threshold is £85,000)

This flowchart offers a step-by-step overview of how to start your IT contracting career, depending on your chosen business structure. By following each stage, you'll have a solid foundation to begin working with UK clients effectively.

Chapter 1 Summary

Starting a career in IT contracting in the UK involves understanding the unique nature of contracting versus permanent employment, choosing the right business structure, and developing in-demand skills. The steps covered in this chapter—from registering your business to obtaining certifications—prepare you for a successful start in the contracting world.

In the next chapter, we'll explore the different business structures in greater depth, helping you determine the best setup based on your goals, preferred working style, and tax efficiency.

Chapter 2

Choosing Your Business Structure

Choosing the right business structure is crucial for any IT contractor, as it determines tax obligations, administrative requirements, and personal liability. The structure you select impacts everything from your income potential to how much time you'll spend on paperwork. This chapter explains the main business structures available for IT contractors in the UK: Limited Company, Umbrella Company, and Sole Trader.

2.1 Overview of Business Structures

In the UK, IT contractors commonly choose between three main business structures:

- **Limited Company**: Contractors set up a private limited company to manage their contracting activities.

- **Umbrella Company**: Contractors join an umbrella company that employs them and manages payroll and taxes.

- **Sole Trader**: Contractors operate as self-employed individuals without forming a company.

Each structure has its unique benefits, tax implications, and administrative requirements.

2.2 Comparing Business Structures: Limited Company vs. Umbrella Company vs. Sole Trader

The table below highlights the differences between the three business structures. Use this comparison to determine which structure aligns best with your financial goals, risk tolerance, and administrative preferences.

Feature	Limited Company	Umbrella Company	Sole Trader
Control	Full control over finances and business decisions	Limited control, payroll managed by umbrella	Full control, but personal liability
Tax Efficiency	Highly tax-efficient, with dividends and expense claims	Limited tax efficiency, all income taxed via PAYE	Limited, with self-assessment tax
IR35 Impact	Can operate outside IR35	Typically, inside IR35	Generally outside IR35, but limited protections
Administrative Burden	High – must handle invoicing, taxes, and filings	Low – umbrella company handles payroll, tax	Moderate – must track income and expenses
Personal Liability	Limited liability protects personal assets	Limited liability through umbrella	Unlimited personal liability
Setup Complexity	High – requires company registration and bank account	Low – join umbrella and start work	Low – register with HMRC for self-assessment
Ideal For	Long-term contractors looking for tax efficiency	Short-term or IR35-compliant roles	Small-scale or part-time contractors

2.3 Setting Up a Limited Company

A Limited Company is often the preferred structure for contractors planning long-term engagements, offering flexibility and tax advantages. However, it comes with greater administrative responsibilities.

Steps to Set Up a Limited Company

1. **Register with Companies House**: Choose a unique name, list directors and shareholders, and complete the registration online. A Certificate of Incorporation will confirm your company's legal formation.

2. **Obtain a Unique Taxpayer Reference (UTR)**: Once registered, HMRC issues a UTR, allowing you to file Corporation Tax returns.

3. **Open a Business Bank Account**: A separate business bank account is essential to manage business finances separately from personal funds.

4. **Appoint an Accountant**: An accountant can assist with VAT, Corporation Tax, and payroll compliance.

5. **Register for VAT (Optional)**: If your turnover exceeds £85,000, you must register for VAT. For lower turnovers, voluntary registration may still offer financial benefits, such as using the Flat Rate VAT scheme.

Benefits of a Limited Company

- **Tax Efficiency**: Contractors can draw a small salary and take dividends, reducing tax liability.

- **Limited Liability**: Personal assets are protected if the business faces financial difficulty.

- **Professional Image**: Limited company status can enhance credibility with clients.

Drawbacks of a Limited Company

- **Administrative Workload**: Requires filing accounts, corporation tax returns, and potentially VAT returns.

- **Director Responsibilities**: You'll be responsible for meeting legal and financial obligations as a director.

2.4 Operating Through an Umbrella Company

For contractors who prefer minimal administration, an umbrella company provides an alternative. The umbrella company employs you, manages payroll, and handles tax deductions, including National Insurance Contributions (NICs) and PAYE.

Joining an Umbrella Company

1. **Choose an Umbrella Provider**: Look for a reputable umbrella company that offers transparent fees and good customer support.

2. **Sign an Employment Contract**: The umbrella company becomes your employer, managing payroll and deducting income tax and NICs on your behalf.

3. **Submit Timesheets and Expenses**: Send your timesheets and claimable expenses (if any) to the umbrella company. They will process your pay after deductions.

4. **Receive PAYE Income**: Your net pay is deposited after tax, NICs, and umbrella fees are deducted.

Benefits of an Umbrella Company

- **No Administration**: Payroll, tax deductions, and insurance are handled for you.

- **IR35 Compliance**: Inside IR35 contracts are more straightforward to manage under an umbrella arrangement.

- **Employment Rights**: You gain certain employee rights, like holiday pay and sick leave.

Drawbacks of an Umbrella Company

- **Limited Tax Efficiency:** All income is taxed at PAYE rates, with no option for dividends.
- **Umbrella Fees:** Service fees reduce overall income.

2.5 Operating as a Sole Trader

As a sole trader, you're self-employed and manage all aspects of your business independently. This structure is easy to set up and is often used by contractors taking on part-time or occasional contracts.

Steps to Register as a Sole Trader

1. **Register with HMRC for Self-Assessment**: Register online for self-assessment. HMRC will issue a UTR to use for tax reporting.

2. **Keep Detailed Records**: Track all business income and expenses to calculate your tax liability.

3. **Manage Your Own Taxes**: Submit an annual self-assessment tax return and pay income tax and NICs on your earnings.

Benefits of Being a Sole Trader

- **Simple Setup**: Registering as a sole trader is quick, requiring only HMRC registration.

- **Full Control**: You retain complete control over business decisions and income.

- **Lower Costs**: No need to pay for company formation or additional tax services.

Drawbacks of Being a Sole Trader

- **Unlimited Liability**: You're personally liable for all business debts, putting your personal assets at risk.

- **Limited Tax Efficiency**: Lacks the tax advantages of a limited company.

- **Reduced Professional Image**: Some clients may prefer limited companies for larger contracts.

2.6 Decision Flowchart: Choosing Your Business Structure

The following flowchart provides a decision guide to help you determine the most suitable business structure for your contracting career.

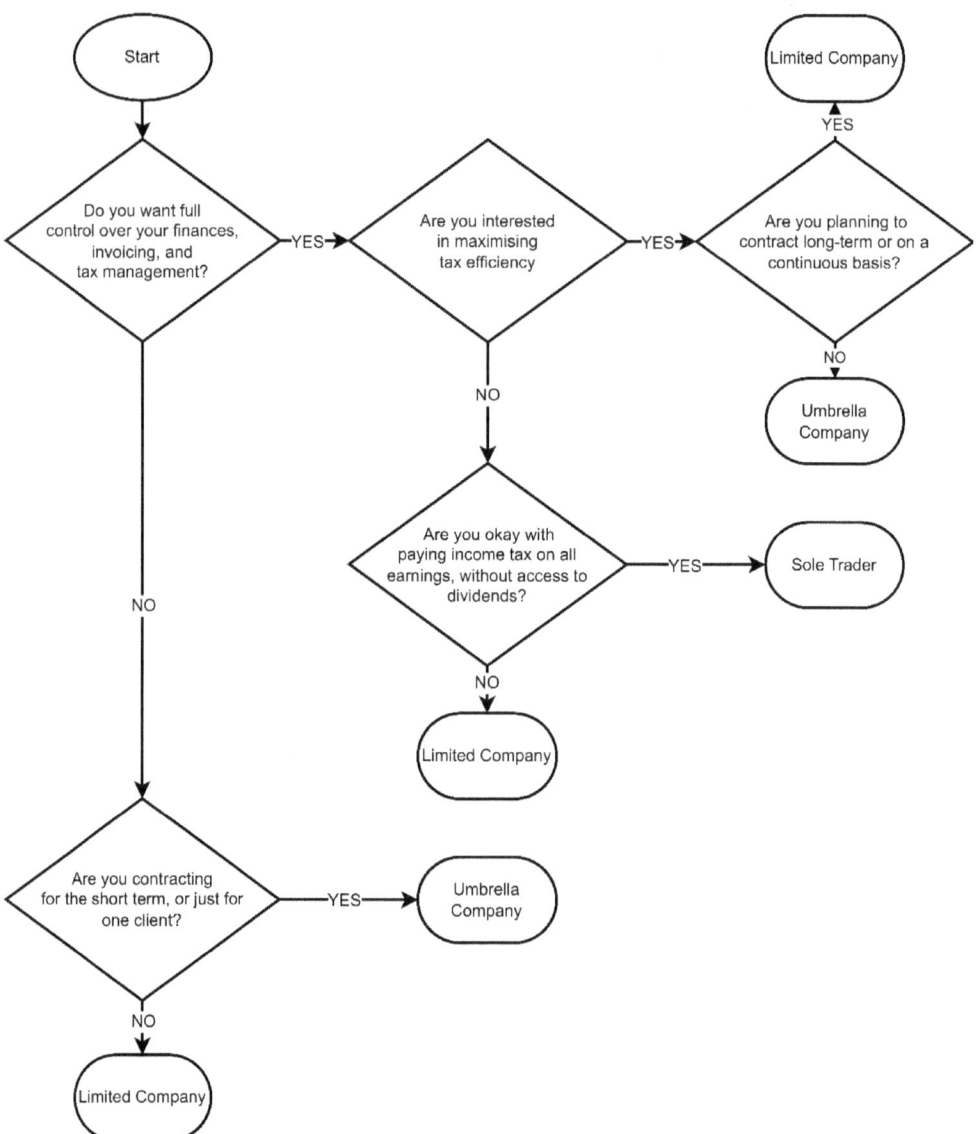

Chapter 2 Summary

Choosing the right business structure is foundational for a successful contracting career. Limited companies offer tax advantages and control but come with more responsibilities. Umbrella companies simplify administration but limit tax efficiency, making them ideal for short-term or inside IR35 contracts. The sole trader route is the simplest, but it involves personal liability and limited tax options.

In the next chapter, we'll explore the UK contracting market, including where to find contract roles, how to market your skills, and tips for securing lucrative projects.

Chapter 3

The Contracting Market in the UK

The UK is one of the most vibrant markets for IT contracting, with high demand for skilled professionals across industries such as finance, healthcare, technology, and government. Understanding market dynamics, knowing where to find contract opportunities, and learning to position yourself effectively are key to building a successful contracting career. This chapter covers the current landscape of the UK contracting market, the types of roles available, and tips for finding and securing contracts.

3.1 Overview of the UK IT Contracting Market

The UK's IT contracting market is driven by several factors:

- **Digital Transformation**: Companies are increasingly investing in digital solutions, fuelling demand for skills in cloud computing, data analytics, AI, and cybersecurity.

- **Skill Shortages**: Many UK companies struggle to find specialised tech skills, making contractors with expertise in high-demand areas highly attractive.

- **Economic Factors**: Economic uncertainty often leads companies to prefer contractors over full-time hires, as contractors provide flexibility and can be brought on for specific projects.

3.2 High-Demand Contracting Roles

Certain IT roles are consistently in high demand in the UK, providing excellent opportunities for contractors with the right skills. Below is a list of the most sought-after contracting roles and their typical requirements.

Role	Description	In-Demand Skills/Certifications
Cybersecurity Specialist	Protects organisations from cyber threats and manages security protocols.	CISSP, CISM, CEH, knowledge of firewalls, intrusion detection
Cloud Architect	Designs and manages cloud infrastructure for scalability and security.	AWS Certified Solutions Architect, Azure Administrator, GCP
Data Scientist	Analyses data to extract insights and support decision-making.	Python, R, SQL, Tableau, machine learning models
Software Developer	Develops, tests, and maintains software applications.	Java, Python, C#, JavaScript, Agile development
Project Manager	Manages project delivery, timelines, and resources.	PMP, PRINCE2, Agile Certified Practitioner, Scrum Master
DevOps Engineer	Integrates development and operations to improve software deployment.	Docker, Kubernetes, Jenkins, AWS, CI/CD pipeline management

These roles represent only a portion of the demand in the UK. Staying informed about emerging technologies and market shifts will help you identify new contracting opportunities.

3.3 Finding Contract Opportunities

To secure IT contracts, it's essential to know where to look. The UK offers numerous channels for contractors to connect with potential clients, from recruitment agencies to online platforms and networking events.

1. Recruitment Agencies Specialising in IT Contracting

Recruitment agencies can be invaluable for contractors. Many agencies specialise in IT and have strong relationships with UK businesses seeking contract talent.

- **Benefits of Using Agencies**: Agencies often have exclusive access to job postings, negotiate contracts, and handle some of the administrative work.

- **Top UK IT Contracting Agencies**: Hays Technology, Nigel Frank, Robert Half Technology, and Lorien offer extensive IT contracting opportunities.

2. Online Job Boards and Freelance Platforms

- **LinkedIn Jobs**: LinkedIn is widely used for networking and finding contract roles. Optimise your profile and connect with recruiters specialising in IT contracting.

- **CWJobs**: CWJobs is a UK-focused job board specifically for IT roles, making it easy to find relevant contract positions.

- **Freelance Platforms**: Websites like Upwork, Toptal, and Freelancer.com provide remote work opportunities, suitable for contractors seeking flexibility or international clients.

3. Direct Outreach and Networking

For experienced contractors, directly reaching out to companies of interest can lead to opportunities. Many companies appreciate proactive communication from skilled contractors who can address specific project needs.

- **Networking Events and Conferences**: Attending industry events like London Tech Week, AI Summit, and Cyber Security Expo helps build connections and identify new opportunities.

- **Professional Associations**: Joining associations like the British Computer Society (BCS) or local tech meetups can expand your network and give access to job boards and industry insights.

3.4 Marketing Yourself as an IT Contractor

Standing out in the competitive contracting market requires effective self-marketing. Here are some essential strategies to promote your skills and experience:

1. Build a Strong LinkedIn Profile
LinkedIn is one of the most powerful tools for IT contractors. Create a profile that highlights your technical skills, certifications, and successful projects.

- **Use Keywords**: Incorporate industry-specific keywords relevant to your role to increase visibility in searches.

- **Showcase Certifications and Projects**: Add certifications and detail project achievements that demonstrate your expertise.

- **Engage with Content**: Share insights on tech trends or post about recent projects (without breaking confidentiality) to showcase knowledge and attract clients.

2. Create a Personal Website or Portfolio
A dedicated website or online portfolio is a great way to display your work, provide testimonials, and detail case studies from previous contracts. Include samples of work, if allowed, or descriptions of past projects to give potential clients an idea of your capabilities.

3. Craft a Tailored CV and Cover Letter
When applying for contracts, tailor your CV to highlight skills relevant to the specific role. In your cover letter, emphasise how your expertise aligns with the client's needs and provide examples of past project successes.

3.5 Tips for Securing Contracts

To maximise your chances of landing high-quality contracts, focus on interview preparation, rate negotiation, and establishing strong client relationships.

Preparing for the Interview

- **Technical Proficiency**: Be prepared to discuss technical details, project outcomes, and relevant skills in depth.

- **Project-Based Examples**: Highlight specific project results, such as efficiency improvements, cost reductions, or process innovations, that demonstrate the impact of your work.

Negotiating Rates and Payment Terms

- **Research Market Rates**: Use resources like ITJobsWatch, Contractor UK, and Hays Salary Guide to understand average rates in your field.

- **Clarify Payment Terms**: Agree on payment frequency (weekly or monthly) and address late payment penalties to avoid cash flow issues.

Building Client Relationships

- **Deliver High-Quality Work**: Consistently deliver results to build credibility, making it more likely for clients to rehire you.

- **Request Feedback and Stay in Touch**: After completing a contract, ask clients for feedback and let them know you're open to future work, as repeat business and referrals are invaluable in contracting.

Below is a representation of key resources for finding contracting roles, organised into categories. This diagram provides a quick reference guide to help you navigate the job search process.

```
┌─────────────────────────────────────────────────────┐
│            Finding Contract Opportunities            │
└─────────────────────────────────────────────────────┘

┌──────────────────┐  ┌──────────────────────┐  ┌──────────────────┐
│   Recruitment    │  │  Online Job Boards & │  │ Direct Outreach &│
│     Agencies     │  │  Freelance Platforms │  │    Networking    │
└──────────────────┘  └──────────────────────┘  └──────────────────┘

┌──────────────────┐  ┌──────────────────────┐  ┌──────────────────┐
│  Hays Technology │  │    LinkedIn Jobs     │  │   Professional   │
│   Nigel Frank    │  │       CWJobs         │  │   Associations   │
│   Robert Half    │  │       Upwork         │  │       (BCS)      │
│    Technology    │  │    Freelancer.com    │  │  Industry Events │
│      Lorien      │  │                      │  │ (London Tech Week)│
└──────────────────┘  └──────────────────────┘  └──────────────────┘
```

3.7 Checklist: Securing Contracts in the UK Market

Here's a checklist to keep you on track as you search for and secure contracts:

- **Identify High-Demand Skills**: Focus on building skills in areas with high demand (e.g., cybersecurity, cloud computing).

- **Leverage Key Platforms**: Use LinkedIn, CWJobs, and relevant freelance platforms regularly to find contracts.

- **Optimise Your LinkedIn Profile**: Include certifications, keywords, and project highlights to attract client interest.

- **Attend Networking Events**: Attend industry conferences, webinars, or meetups to meet potential clients and peers.

- **Prepare a Tailored CV**: Emphasise relevant skills and accomplishments specific to each contract application.

- **Negotiate Rates Confidently**: Research average rates and understand your value to secure fair compensation.

- **Stay in Touch with Past Clients**: Build lasting relationships and maintain contact to open doors for future opportunities.

Chapter 3 Summary

The UK contracting market offers a wealth of opportunities for IT professionals with specialised skills. By understanding high-demand roles, leveraging the right platforms, and refining your marketing approach, you can position yourself effectively in this competitive market. Keep networking, continually improve your skills, and build strong client relationships to ensure long-term success.

In the next chapter, we'll cover IR35 legislation and tax implications, helping you understand how to navigate UK tax requirements and remain compliant.

Chapter 4

IR35 Legislation and Tax Implications

IR35 legislation is a critical consideration for IT contractors in the UK, as it directly impacts tax liabilities and income. Introduced to prevent "disguised employment," IR35 assesses whether contractors are genuinely self-employed or operating as employees for tax purposes. This chapter explains IR35, its implications, and how to determine your IR35 status. We'll also cover strategies for managing your finances within IR35 compliance and include visual aids to help you navigate this complex legislation.

4.1 Understanding IR35

IR35, was introduced by HMRC to tackle cases where contractors operate through intermediaries (e.g., limited companies) but function as employees, thus benefiting from tax advantages.

- **Inside IR35**: If a contract is inside IR35, HMRC considers the contractor a "disguised employee," and they must pay employment-like taxes (PAYE and NICs).

- **Outside IR35**: If a contract is outside IR35, the contractor is considered self-employed and can pay themselves through dividends and claim business expenses.

Key Factors for IR35 Determination

IR35 status is determined based on three main criteria:

- **Control**: Who controls the work—does the client dictate how, when, and where work is performed?
- **Substitution**: Can the contractor send a substitute to complete the work, or is the service personally required?
- **Mutuality of Obligation (MOO)**: Is there an ongoing obligation for the client to offer work and for the contractor to accept it?

4.2 Tax Implications of IR35

The tax treatment for contractors depends on whether they fall inside or outside IR35. Below is a breakdown of the implications for each IR35 status.

Inside IR35
- **PAYE Income Tax and NICs:** Contractors are taxed at employment rates, reducing take-home pay.
- **No Dividend Payments:** Contractors must take all income as salary, which is fully taxable.
- **Restricted Expenses:** No allowable expenses for travel and subsistence under IR35.

Outside IR35
- **Salary and Dividends**: Contractors can structure their income as a combination of salary and dividends, with dividends taxed at a lower rate.
- **Allowable Expenses**: Contractors can claim tax-deductible business expenses, such as travel, accommodation, and training.
- **Higher Take-Home Pay**: Reduced tax rates and allowable expenses lead to a higher net income.

Tax Treatment	Inside IR35	Outside IR35
Income	Entire income through PAYE	Combination of salary and dividends
NICs	Employee and employer NICs apply	NICs only on salary
Tax-Deductible Expenses	Limited expenses	Full range of business expenses allowed
Take-Home Pay	Lower due to higher taxes	Higher due to tax efficiency

4.3 Determining Your IR35 Status

Determining your IR35 status requires assessing the nature of your working relationship with each client. HMRC uses various "tests of employment" to evaluate contracts.

1. Control

- If the client has significant control over how, where, and when the work is done, the contract is more likely to be inside IR35.
- Contractors with control over work location, hours, and methods have a stronger case for being outside IR35.

2. Substitution

- The right to provide a substitute (another person to complete the work) supports an outside IR35 determination.
- If the client expects the work to be performed solely by you, the contract may be inside IR35.

3. Mutuality of Obligation (MOO)

- If the client is obliged to provide work and the contractor is obliged to accept it, this points to an employment relationship (inside IR35).
- Outside IR35 relationships often specify that the contractor is only required to complete specific tasks within the contract's scope.

4.4 Using HMRC's CEST Tool

HMRC offers the **Check Employment Status for Tax (CEST)** tool to help contractors and clients assess IR35 status. This online tool provides guidance on IR35 status based on questions about the working arrangement.

How to Use the CEST Tool

1. **Access CEST Tool**: Visit HMRC's website and locate the CEST tool.

2. **Answer Questions**: Provide information about the contract, including control, substitution, and MOO factors.

3. **Review Results**: The tool will indicate whether the contract is likely inside or outside IR35. However, HMRC doesn't guarantee results, and contractors may still be subject to audit.

4.5 Managing IR35 Compliance

To remain compliant with IR35, contractors can take proactive steps to avoid being incorrectly classified as inside IR35 and to protect themselves from financial penalties.

1. Contract Review

- Have a specialist review your contract to ensure it reflects an outside IR35 status if applicable. Contracts should emphasise contractor autonomy and explicitly allow for substitution.

2. Use IR35 Insurance

- Consider IR35 insurance, which covers the cost of a tax investigation and potential liabilities if HMRC challenges your status. This is especially useful for high-value contracts.

3. Maintain Supporting Documentation

- Keep records of correspondence with clients, especially details that support your autonomy, substitution rights, and specific project-based work.

4. Seek Professional Advice

- Consulting with an IR35 specialist or tax advisor can help you understand your status and avoid costly mistakes. They can assist with contract reviews, tax planning, and compliance strategies.

4.6 Checklist: Staying Compliant with IR35

Here's a checklist to help you stay on top of your IR35 status and remain compliant:

- **Review Contracts Carefully**: Confirm contracts include clauses that support an outside IR35 status.

- **Use the CEST Tool for Guidance**: Assess each contract with the CEST tool but be cautious about over-relying on it.

- **Consult an IR35 Specialist**: Get professional advice to reduce risk and clarify status.

- **Document Client Interactions**: Keep records of any agreements or communications that affirm your independent status.

- **Consider IR35 Insurance**: Protect yourself financially in case of an HMRC investigation.

Chapter 4 Summary

IR35 is complex legislation that requires careful management by UK contractors to avoid unexpected tax obligations and maintain financial stability. By understanding IR35's key tests—control, substitution, and mutuality of obligation—you can better assess your contracts and take necessary steps to ensure compliance. From using the CEST tool to consulting with IR35 specialists, there are resources and strategies available to support you in navigating IR35.

In the next chapter, we'll explore essential financial management practices for contractors, including budgeting, invoicing, and tax planning to maximise income and ensure smooth financial operations.

Chapter 5

Taxes, Accounting, and Financial Management for Contractors

Efficient financial management is essential for IT contractors in the UK, as it impacts profitability, tax compliance, and the long-term sustainability of your business. This chapter delves into the latest HMRC tax guidelines, essential accounting practices, and financial planning strategies tailored for contractors. By mastering these areas, you'll be well-equipped to maximise your income, minimise tax liabilities, and stay compliant with current regulations.

5.1 Understanding Your Tax Obligations

As a contractor, your tax obligations differ significantly from those of salaried employees. Your specific responsibilities will depend on your chosen business structure—whether you operate as a Limited Company, work through an Umbrella Company, or are a Sole Trader.

Key Tax Obligations for UK Contractors

1. Income Tax
- **Limited Company**: Contractors usually take a small salary to reduce National Insurance Contributions (NICs) and receive the remainder of income as dividends, which are subject to different tax rates.
- **Sole Trader**: Pays income tax on all profits through the self-assessment process.
- **Umbrella Company**: Income tax is deducted via PAYE (Pay As You Earn), similar to traditional employees, simplifying tax compliance but reducing overall take-home pay.

2. Corporation Tax
- **Limited Company**: Corporation tax applies to company profits. As of the 2023/24 tax year, the main corporation tax rate is 25% for companies with profits above £50,000, and a "small profits rate" of 19% applies to profits up to £50,000. Companies with profits between £50,000 and £250,000 are taxed at a tapered rate.
    - **Planning Tip**: Contractors can reduce their taxable profits by claiming allowable business expenses and using deductions like pension contributions and equipment costs.

3. Dividend Tax
- Dividends are subject to lower tax rates than salary income. The dividend allowance for the 2023/24 tax year is £1,000 (down from £2,000 in previous years), meaning you pay no tax on the first £1,000 of dividends. Above this, dividend tax rates are:
    - 8.75% for basic rate taxpayers
    - 33.75% for higher-rate taxpayers
    - 39.35% for additional rate taxpayers

4. VAT (Value Added Tax)
- If your turnover exceeds £85,000, VAT registration is mandatory, but you may also voluntarily register below this threshold to reclaim VAT on business expenses.
- **Flat Rate VAT Scheme**: Many contractors use the Flat Rate Scheme to simplify VAT calculations. With this scheme, you pay a fixed rate (typically around 14.5% for IT consultants) on your gross turnover, keeping any difference between the VAT you charge clients, and the amount owed to HMRC.

5. National Insurance Contributions (NICs)
- **Limited Company**: NICs are typically paid on the small salary you take, not on dividends. This strategy reduces NIC liability, increasing your overall take-home pay.
- **Sole Trader**: Pays both Class 2 and Class 4 NICs, calculated as part of the self-assessment tax return.

5.2 Essential Accounting Practices for Contractors

Accurate and organised accounting is essential to keep your finances under control, ensure compliance, and prepare for tax filings. Here's what you need to focus on as a contractor.

1. Bookkeeping Basics

- **Income and Expense Tracking**: Use dedicated accounting software to record all income and expenses. Tools like **QuickBooks, FreeAgent,** and **Xero** help categorise expenses and monitor cash flow in real-time.

- **Separate Business Account**: Open a dedicated business bank account to keep your personal and business finances separate. This will simplify tracking expenses and making it easier to claim allowable expenses.

2. Invoicing Best Practices

- **Professional Invoices**: Include your business name, address, VAT registration number (if applicable), client details, and a clear description of services provided.

- **Payment Terms**: Set clear terms, typically Net 30 or Net 15, to ensure a steady cash flow. Consider using invoicing tools within software like **Xero** or **FreshBooks** to automate invoices and track payment statuses.

3. Managing and Claiming Expenses

- **Allowable Expenses**: HMRC allows you to deduct expenses that are "wholly, exclusively, and necessarily" for business purposes. Common expenses include travel, office supplies, and professional training.

- **Digital Receipts**: Keep a record of all receipts for at least six years, as HMRC may request them in case of an audit. Use tools like **Expensify** to scan and organise receipts digitally, ensuring easy access when needed.

Expense Category	Examples of Allowable Expenses
Office Supplies	Computers, software, peripherals, and office equipment
Travel	Business mileage, train tickets, hotel stays (no commuting costs)
Training and Courses	Certifications or courses directly related to your work
Home Office	A portion of household bills (electricity, internet, etc.)
Professional Fees	Accountancy, business insurance, and industry memberships

This table highlights expenses that can be deducted to reduce taxable income, helping contractors increase their profit margins.

5.3 Financial Planning and Budgeting

Proper financial planning allows contractors to maintain stability, handle tax obligations, and prepare for periods between contracts. Here are some critical strategies.

1. Setting Aside Tax Funds
- **Allocate for Taxes**: As a contractor, taxes aren't automatically deducted, so it's essential to set aside a portion of each payment (usually 20-30%) to cover income tax, NICs, and VAT. Consider using a dedicated savings account for tax funds.

2. Budgeting for Gaps Between Contracts
- **Build a Reserve Fund**: Income fluctuations are common in contracting, so a savings buffer of 3-6 months of expenses is recommended to cover potential gaps between contracts.
- **Track Cash Flow**: Regularly review cash flow to anticipate financial needs and prevent overspending. Budgeting tools like **You Need a Budget (YNAB)** can be helpful for monitoring cash flow and expenses.

3. Planning for Retirement
- **Pension Contributions**: Contractors can set up a Self-Invested Personal Pension (SIPP), which can be funded from company profits. This allows for tax-efficient contributions that reduce your Corporation Tax liability.
- **ISAs and Other Investments**: Individual Savings Accounts (ISAs) provide a tax-free way to grow savings outside of a pension. Consider diversifying with both ISAs and pensions to build long-term financial security.

The graphic below helps visualise typical cash inflows and outflows, clearly showing essential expenses and income sources.

Monthly Cash Inflows
- Contract Income
- Other Business Income
  (consulting, freelance work)

Monthly Cash Outflows
- Taxes (income tax, VAT, NICs
- Business Expenses
  (equipment, software, travel)
- Pension Contributions
- Personal Draw
  (salary, dividends)

5.4 Tax Efficiency: The Salary and Dividend Strategy

Operating as a Limited Company allows contractors to use a combination of salary and dividends to maximise tax efficiency.

Setting a Minimal Salary

- Taking a salary just above the Lower Earnings Limit for NICs (currently £12,570) provides access to state benefits while minimising NICs.

Using Dividends

- Dividends are taxed at lower rates than salary, making them a tax-efficient way to pay yourself. In the 2023/24 tax year, the tax-free dividend allowance is £1,000. Above this threshold, dividends are taxed at:
    - 8.75% for basic rate
    - 33.75% for higher rate
    - 39.35% for additional rate

Income Type	Tax Rate	Benefits
Salary	Subject to income tax and NICs	Builds NIC contributions for state benefits
Dividends	Lower tax rates post-allowance	Increases tax efficiency, reduces NIC burden

The table above shows the potential benefits of using dividends in combination with a minimal salary for optimal tax efficiency.

5.5 Essential Accounting and Financial Tools

Effective financial tools simplify accounting, invoicing, and tracking expenses. Here are some tools particularly useful for contractors:

1. Accounting Software

- **QuickBooks**: Offers VAT tracking, invoicing, and expense management.
- **FreeAgent**: Designed for UK contractors, it supports VAT, invoicing, and integrates with HMRC's Making Tax Digital system.
- **Xero**: Supports multi-currency accounting, ideal for contractors working with international clients.

2. Expense Tracking and Invoicing

- **Toggl**: A simple time-tracking tool for hourly or project-based contractors.
- **Expensify**: Allows contractors to scan receipts and automate expense tracking, reducing manual data entry.

3. Budgeting and Tax Calculators

- **TaxScouts**: Provides a tax-filing service for contractors, with advisory options for complex tax questions.
- **You Need A Budget (YNAB)**: Helps contractors set budgets, track expenses, and build savings.

Financial Tools Matrix

Tool	Function	Best For
QuickBooks	Accounting, VAT, invoicing	Comprehensive financial management
FreeAgent	UK-specific tax and invoicing	Contractors needing VAT and MTD support
Toggl	Time tracking for invoicing	Contractors billing hourly or by project
Expensify	Automated expense tracking	Scanning and organising receipts

This matrix highlights tools that can streamline financial management, ensuring compliance and accuracy.

5.6 Checklist: Effective Financial Management for Contractors

This checklist consolidates the key financial management practices for UK contractors, helping you stay organised and compliant.

- **Set Up a Dedicated Business Account**: Keep personal and business finances separate.

- **Use Accounting Software**: Track income, expenses, and VAT to streamline tax filing.

- **Invoice Clients Promptly**: Set clear payment terms and follow up on overdue invoices.

- **Save for Taxes and Compliance**: Allocate funds for income tax, VAT, and NICs.

- **Optimise Salary and Dividends**: Balance between the two for maximum tax efficiency.

- **Maintain Accurate Records**: Store receipts and records for at least six years.

- **Plan for Retirement**: Use tax-efficient pension contributions and other investments.

The checklist below serves as a high-level summary of essential steps for effective financial management.

Financial Management Checklist
1. Set Up a Business Bank Account
2. Use Accounting Software
3. Invoice Clients Promptly
4. Allocate Funds for Tax Liabilities
5. Optimize Salary and Dividends for Tax Efficiency
6. Maintain Financial Records
7. Plan for Retirement and Investments

Chapter 5 Summary

Mastering taxes, accounting, and financial management is essential for every UK IT contractor. By understanding your tax obligations, setting up efficient accounting practices, and leveraging the latest HMRC guidelines, you can maximise your earnings, stay compliant, and build a sustainable contracting career. Implement the strategies and tools from this chapter to establish a strong financial foundation, setting yourself up for long-term success.

In the next chapter, we'll dive into managing contracts and client relationships, exploring contract negotiation, building strong client connections, and handling challenging situations professionally.

Chapter 6

Managing Contracts and Clients

Successful contract management and strong client relationships are essential for IT contractors. Each project brings new expectations, requirements, and timelines, and managing these effectively can mean the difference between securing repeat business and struggling to find consistent work. This chapter covers essential strategies for setting up contracts, managing client expectations, and handling potential conflicts. Visual aids, including a sample contract outline and a client management checklist, will help clarify best practices for managing contracts and building positive client relationships.

6.1 Setting Up a Clear Contract

A well-defined contract establishes the foundation for a successful client relationship. It protects both parties by clearly outlining the project's scope, responsibilities, payment terms, and other essential details.

Key Components of an IT Contract

1. **Scope of Work (SOW)**: Define the specific tasks, deliverables, and milestones. Clearly state what's included—and, importantly, what's excluded—to prevent scope creep.

2. **Payment Terms**: Outline the agreed rate (hourly, daily, or project-based), payment schedule, and payment terms (e.g., Net 30 days). Consider penalties for late payments to ensure timely compensation.

3. **Intellectual Property (IP) and Confidentiality**: Specify who owns the intellectual property for the work and include a confidentiality clause to protect sensitive information.

4. **Termination Clause**: Include conditions for ending the contract early, including any required notice period and applicable fees.

5. **Governing Law**: State the applicable legal jurisdiction in case of disputes, which is particularly important for international contracts.

The contract outline below, serves as a reference, ensuring that all essential components are included in every client agreement.

Sample IT Contract

1. Scope of Work (SOW)
   - List of tasks, deliverables, and exclusions
2. Payment Terms
   - Rate, invoicing frequency, and payment schedule
3. Intellectual Property and Confidentiality
   - IP ownership and data confidentiality terms
4. Termination Clause
   - Conditions for early contract termination
5. Governing Law
   - Legal jurisdiction in case of disputes

6.2 Setting Client Expectations

Managing expectations from the beginning of a project helps prevent misunderstandings, promotes satisfaction, and fosters trust.

Steps to Set Clear Expectations with Clients

1. **Define Project Goals and Milestones**: In initial meetings, clarify the project's goals, deliverables, and timelines. If the project has milestones, agree on specific dates for each phase.

2. **Communicate Your Availability**: Specify your work hours, response times, and any days you won't be available. Setting these boundaries early helps clients understand when they can expect updates.

3. **Specify Revision Limits**: State how many revisions are included in the contract and the process for requesting them. This minimises the risk of clients expecting unlimited changes.

4. **Regular Check-Ins**: Schedule periodic progress reviews with the client to discuss updates, challenges, and any potential changes in scope.

6.3 Negotiating Contract Terms

Effective negotiation can protect your interests, increase your earnings, and create a more positive working relationship. Here are some tips for negotiating favourable terms:

1. Know Your Worth
- Research market rates for similar roles to determine a fair rate. Websites like ITJobsWatch and Contractor UK provide insights into average contractor rates by skill and region.

2. Set Clear Payment Terms
- **Upfront Deposits**: To secure your income, consider requesting an upfront deposit or milestone-based payments for large or long-term projects.
- **Payment Schedule**: Common options are weekly, bi-weekly, or monthly. Make sure payment terms are clearly outlined in the contract.

3. Limit Scope Creep
- Clearly define the scope of work in the contract and specify additional fees for extra work beyond the agreed scope. Use a change order process for any out-of-scope requests.

4. Protect Intellectual Property
- Ensure the contract states that intellectual property rights transfer to the client only upon full payment. This protects your rights if the client does not complete payment.

The visual below serves as a quick reference for key negotiation points, helping you secure terms that protect your interests.

Contract Negotiation Tips

1. Know Your Market Rate:
    - Research rates in your field to set fair pricing

2. Request Upfront Deposits for Long Projects

3. Limit Scope Creep
    - Clearly define scope and add a change order clause

4. Protect Intellectual Property
    - Ensure IP transfers only after full payment

6.4 Building Strong Client Relationships

Building rapport with clients not only fosters trust but also increases the chances of repeat business and referrals. Here's how to develop a positive relationship with each client.

1. Communicate Regularly

- Keep clients updated with regular progress reports, even if there are no major changes. This shows transparency and keeps clients informed.

2. Deliver on Promises

- Consistently meet deadlines, deliver high-quality work, and demonstrate reliability. Exceeding client expectations can result in positive feedback and repeat projects.

3. Be Proactive and Solution-Oriented

- If you foresee potential issues, address them with the client proactively. Offering solutions rather than just highlighting problems showcases your professionalism and problem-solving skills.

4. Request Feedback

- After completing a project, ask for client feedback to identify areas for improvement. Positive testimonials from satisfied clients can also enhance your credibility.

The visual below offers a clear list of relationship-building strategies, which can be used as a checklist to ensure successful client interactions.

Building Strong Client Relationships

1. Communicate Regularly
   - Keep clients updated with progress reports

2. Deliver on Promises
   - Meet deadlines and exceed expectations if possible

3. Be Proactive and Solution-Oriented

4. Request Feedback and Use Testimonials

6.5 Handling Client Conflicts and Difficult Situations

Conflicts may arise over timelines, deliverables, or misunderstandings. Managing these conflicts professionally can help resolve issues quickly and maintain a positive relationship.

1. Address Issues Early

- When a problem arises, discuss it with the client as soon as possible. Avoiding issues only worsens them over time.

2. Listen and Understand the Client's Perspective

- Make an effort to understand the client's concerns, which will make them feel valued and help you identify practical solutions.

3. Offer Solutions, Not Excuses

- Instead of focusing on what went wrong, propose actionable solutions. If a deadline is at risk, offer a revised timeline.

4. Document Resolutions

- After resolving any conflict, summarise the agreement in writing. This ensures that both parties understand the solution and prevents future misunderstandings.

This visual below offers a straightforward approach to handling client conflicts, emphasising proactive communication and solutions.

Conflict Resolution Steps

1. Address Issues Early
    - Discuss problems as soon as they arise
2. Listen and Understand Client's Perspective
    - Meet deadlines and exceed expectations if possible
3. Offer Solutions Instead of Excuses
    - Focus on actionable solutions
4. Document Resolutions
    - Summarize agreements in writing

6.6 Client Management Tools

There are various tools that contractors can use to streamline client management, handle contracts, and maintain strong communication.

Popular Client Management Tools

- **CRM Software**: Customer Relationship Management (CRM) tools like HubSpot or Zoho help you track client information, project status, and follow-ups.

- **Project Management Software**: Tools like Trello, Asana, and Monday.com help organise tasks, manage deadlines, and provide updates to client updates.

- **Invoicing Software**: FreshBooks and QuickBooks simplify invoicing and help you track payment status, ensuring timely payments.

Tool	Purpose	Ideal For
HubSpot CRM	Client information tracking	Managing client contacts and follow-ups
Trello	Task and project management	Tracking project progress and deadlines
QuickBooks	Invoicing and financial tracking	Simplifying billing and cash flow
Slack	Real-time communication	Maintaining ongoing communication

This matrix helps you select the right client management tools based on your workflow and communication needs.

6.7 Checklist: Effective Client and Contract Management

Use this checklist to ensure your client and contract management practices are efficient and professional:

- **Set Clear Contract Terms**: Ensure every contract includes scope, payment terms, IP rights, and a termination clause.

- **Establish Communication Protocols**: Set expectations for response times, preferred communication methods, and regular updates.

- **Document Client Interactions**: Keep records of all client interactions, especially agreements on project scope or changes.

- **Follow Up on Payments Promptly**: Use invoicing software to track outstanding payments and send reminders if necessary.

- **Request Feedback After Completion**: Use client feedback for improvement and testimonials for future marketing.

Chapter 6 Summary

Managing contracts and clients effectively is essential for IT contractors who want to build a strong reputation and ensure project success. By setting clear expectations, negotiating favourable terms, and maintaining professional client relationships, you create a foundation for long-term success. The tools, strategies, and visual aids in this chapter will help you streamline contract management, communicate effectively with clients, and handle conflicts professionally.

In the next chapter, we'll discuss essential tools and techniques for IT contractors, covering project management, communication, and financial management software that can streamline your workflow and increase productivity.

Chapter 7

Working with Agencies

Working with recruitment agencies is a popular strategy for IT contractors looking to secure consistent projects and connect with reputable clients. Agencies can simplify the job search, manage contracts, and help navigate administrative tasks. However, it's essential to understand how to work effectively with agencies, negotiate terms, and choose agencies that align with your career goals. This chapter will cover the benefits and challenges of working with agencies, how to select the right agency, and tips for managing these relationships. Visual aids, including a workflow for finding and securing contracts through agencies and a checklist for evaluating agencies, will guide you through the process.

7.1 Understanding the Role of Agencies in IT Contracting

Recruitment agencies act as intermediaries between contractors and clients. They specialise in connecting contractors with companies needing temporary or project-based expertise. Here's a breakdown of how agencies typically operate and their primary roles.

Roles of Recruitment Agencies
- **Job Sourcing**: Agencies have a network of clients and often access to unadvertised roles, making it easier to find projects quickly.
- **Contract Negotiation**: Agencies handle rate discussions, contract terms, and can negotiate on behalf of the contractor.
- **Administrative Support**: Many agencies manage payroll, invoicing, and compliance, especially for contractors working under IR35 or inside umbrella companies.

Advantages of Working with Agencies
1. **Access to Exclusive Opportunities**: Many companies rely exclusively on agencies to fill certain roles, so contractors working with agencies may access roles they couldn't find elsewhere.
2. **Time Savings**: Agencies handle contract sourcing, client interactions, and administrative processes, allowing contractors to focus on project delivery.
3. **Contract Protection**: Reputable agencies ensure contracts are legally sound and compliant, offering an added layer of security for contractors.

Challenges of Working with Agencies

- **Service Fees**: Agencies take a percentage of the contract value as their fee, which can reduce your earnings.

- **Less Direct Control**: Contractors may have less control over contract terms and negotiation when working through agencies.

- **Potential Exclusivity Clauses**: Some agencies require exclusivity, limiting a contractor's ability to seek other roles independently.

7.2 Choosing the Right Agency

Not all agencies are the same, and choosing one that aligns with your professional goals can impact your contracting experience. Here's how to evaluate and select a recruitment agency.

Factors to Consider When Choosing an Agency

1. **Industry Specialisation**: Agencies focused on IT contracting or your specific field (e.g., cybersecurity, software development) are more likely to understand the unique needs of your expertise.

2. **Reputation and Reviews**: Research the agency's reputation by reading online reviews and speaking to other contractors. Look for agencies known for fair terms, reliable payment, and strong client relationships.

3. **Support Services**: Evaluate what additional services the agency offers, such as IR35 guidance, payroll support, or assistance with invoicing.

4. **Transparency of Fees**: Ensure the agency is transparent about fees and markup. The industry average is typically 10-30%, so be cautious of agencies with high fees or hidden costs.

5. **Contract Type**: Some agencies specialise in long-term placements, while others focus on short-term or project-based contracts. Choose one that aligns with your preferred contract duration.

The checklist below simplifies the process of evaluating agencies, ensuring that you select one with a strong reputation and relevant services.

Agency Evaluation Checklist

1. Industry Specialisation
    - Does the agency focus on IT or your field?
2. Reputation and Reviews
    - Check online reviews and ask for recommendations
3. Support Services
    - Do they provide IR35, payroll, or compliance help?
4. Transparency of Fees
    - Are fees reasonable and clearly explained?
5. Contract Type
    - Do they offer contracts that match your goals?

7.3 Understanding Contract Types and IR35 Compliance

When working through an agency, it's essential to understand how contract types impact IR35 status and earnings. IR35 compliance determines if you are considered a self-employed contractor or a "disguised employee" for tax purposes.

Contract Types
- **Outside IR35 Contracts**: Contracts considered "outside IR35" allow contractors to operate as independent businesses. You can take advantage of tax benefits by combining salary and dividends.
- **Inside IR35 Contracts**: Contracts "inside IR35" mean that HMRC considers the contractor akin to an employee for tax purposes, which affects how income is taxed.
- **Umbrella Contracts**: Some agencies require contractors to use an umbrella company, which manages PAYE tax and NICs on your behalf, making it easier to handle inside IR35 contracts.

Contract Type	IR35 Status	Tax Implications	Ideal For
Outside IR35	Self-employed	Combination of salary and dividends	Independent contractors
Inside IR35	"Disguised employee"	PAYE tax, no dividend payments	Long-term, employee-like roles
Umbrella Contract	Managed by umbrella	PAYE tax through umbrella company	Simplified for inside IR35

This table helps contractors understand the differences between contract types and how they align with IR35 requirements.

7.4 Navigating the Agency Relationship

Establishing a productive relationship with an agency can lead to more consistent work, favourable contract terms, and even higher rates. Here are tips for maintaining a successful agency relationship:

1. Communicate Clearly

- From the start, communicate your skills, availability, and preferred project types. Clear communication helps the agency find projects that align with your goals.

2. Set Expectations on Payment and Terms

- Ensure that payment terms, invoicing cycles, and payment timelines are clearly outlined. If the agency handles payroll, confirm when payments are expected and any associated fees.

3. Be Responsive and Professional

- Agencies appreciate contractors who respond quickly and meet deadlines. Consistently professional behaviour strengthens your reputation and increases the likelihood of future placements.

4. Provide Feedback

- Offer feedback to the agency about each contract. Letting them know what worked well and any challenges helps the agency understand your preferences for future roles.

This visual guide provides a simple checklist for building a positive and lasting relationship with an agency.

Tips for a Strong Agency Relationship

1. Communicate Clearly
   - Define skills, availability, and project goals
2. Confirm Payment Terms
   - Review payment cycle, fees, and invoicing
3. Be Responsive and Professional
   - Timely communication and meeting deadlines
4. Provide Feedback
   - Share insights to improve future contracts

7.5 Negotiating Terms with Agencies

Even though agencies handle much of the negotiation process, it's important to advocate for favourable terms. Here's how to negotiate effectively:

1. Know Your Market Rate

- Research industry rates for your skills and experience level. Resources like ITJobsWatch and Contractor UK offer insights into current rates by skill and region.

2. Request Transparency on Agency Markup

- Agencies add a markup on top of your rate when billing clients. Knowing the total rate billed to the client helps you understand the agency's fees and assess if you're receiving fair compensation.

3. Set Payment Terms That Support Cash Flow

- Aim for shorter payment cycles, such as 14 days, to improve cash flow. Some agencies may agree to quicker terms, especially for high-demand skills.

4. Discuss Scope and Additional Charges

- Clarify the project scope and agree on charges for out-of-scope work to avoid unexpected demands that aren't compensated.

This checklist provides an easy-to-reference guide to negotiating terms with agencies, ensuring you secure fair and beneficial contract terms.

Key Negotiation Points
1. Know Your Market Rate   - Research rates based on skill and region
2. Ask for Transparency on Agency Markup   - Understand the agency's fees
3. Set Favourable Payment Terms   - Shorter payment cycles support cash flow
4. Clarify Scope of Work and Additional Charges   - Avoid unpaid extra work

7.6 Advantages and Disadvantages of Agency Work

Working with agencies has pros and cons. Understanding these can help you decide if agency work aligns with your contracting goals.

Advantages of Agency Work

- **Quick Access to Roles**: Agencies often have immediate openings, which reduces downtime between contracts.
- **Reduced Administrative Burden**: Agencies handle contract details, client communication, and payroll (if using an umbrella).
- **Opportunity to Build a Client Network**: Contractors can build relationships with multiple clients, creating future opportunities.

Disadvantages of Agency Work

- **Reduced Earnings Due to Fees**: Agency fees can lower net income.
- **Less Control Over Terms**: Contractors may have limited ability to negotiate rates or terms directly with the client.
- **Potential Exclusivity Clauses**: Some agencies require contractors to work only through them for specified clients or projects.

Advantages	Disadvantages
Access to exclusive roles	Reduced earnings due to agency fees
Reduced admin tasks	Limited control over contract terms
Easier client management	Possible exclusivity requirements

This table summarises the benefits and drawbacks of agency work.

7.7 Checklist: Working Effectively with Agencies

Here's a checklist to keep you organised and prepared when working with agencies:

- **Research Agency Reputation**: Look for reputable agencies with positive reviews.

- **Define Your Project Preferences**: Specify your preferred contract duration, field, and skills.

- **Clarify Payment Terms and Cycle**: Ensure you understand the payment terms, cycle, and any agency fees.

- **Negotiate for Transparency**: Ask the agency about its markup and ensure your rate is fair.

- **Maintain Professional Communication**: Be responsive, professional, and open to feedback.

Chapter 7 Summary

Working with agencies can provide a steady flow of contracts and simplify the contracting process. By understanding agency roles, evaluating their services, and maintaining a professional relationship, you can benefit from agency connections while protecting your interests. This chapter's visual aids and checklists offer practical strategies for finding the right agency, negotiating favourable terms, and building strong agency relationships.

In the next chapter, we'll dive into essential tools and techniques for IT contractors, covering project management, communication, and financial management software to streamline your workflow and increase productivity.

Chapter 8

Essential Tools and Techniques for IT Contractors

The right tools and techniques can streamline project management, simplify financial tracking, and improve communication with clients and agencies. From time-tracking apps to project management platforms, these tools help you stay organised and efficient. In this chapter, we'll cover key tools and techniques that every IT contractor should consider, along with visual aids to guide you in choosing the most effective solutions for your needs.

8.1 Time Tracking and Billing Tools

Accurate time tracking and billing are essential for contractors, especially for those who work on an hourly or daily rate. These tools help you track your work hours and ensure timely invoicing.

Popular Time Tracking and Billing Tools
- **Toggl:** Toggl is a user-friendly time tracking tool that provides insights into your work patterns. It's ideal for logging hours on multiple projects and generating reports.
- **Harvest:** Harvest offers time tracking with invoicing features. It integrates with project management tools like Asana and Trello, and allows contractors to invoice directly from the app.
- **Clockify:** Clockify is a free tool with unlimited tracking and reporting features, ideal for independent contractors on a budget.

Best Practices for Time Tracking
- **Track Time Daily:** Log hours as you work to ensure accuracy.
- **Categorise by Project:** Use tags to organise time entries by project, making it easy to view hours spent on each contract.
- **Generate Weekly Reports:** Send weekly time reports to clients, which keeps them updated and encourages timely payments.

Tool	Features	Ideal For
Toggl	Time tracking, reporting	Simple tracking across projects
Harvest	Time tracking, invoicing	Integrated time and billing solutions
Clockify	Free tracking, unlimited reports	Budget-conscious contractors

This table helps you quickly identify the best time tracking and billing tool based on your needs.

8.2 Project Management Tools

Project management tools help contractors track deadlines, organise tasks, and manage communication with clients. These tools can be particularly helpful when juggling multiple projects with different clients.

Popular Project Management Tools
- **Trello**: Trello uses boards and cards to organise tasks visually. It's ideal for simple projects and tracking progress at a glance.
- **Asana**: Asana offers task management with more advanced features, including project timelines and dependencies, making it suitable for complex, multi-step projects.
- **Jira**: Built for IT and software projects, Jira provides features tailored for agile development, making it ideal for contractors working on sprints and iterative projects.

Best Practices for Project Management
- **Set Milestones**: Break projects into milestones to provide clear targets and allow clients to see progress.
- **Prioritise Tasks**: Organise tasks by priority to ensure that critical deliverables are completed on time.
- **Regular Check-Ins**: Schedule periodic updates with clients to align on progress and address any potential issues.

Tool	Primary Features	Best For
Trello	Visual boards, task cards	Simple, visual project tracking
Asana	Task assignments, timelines, calendar	Multi-step, collaborative projects
Jira	Agile sprints, issue tracking	Software development and IT projects

This visual aid simplifies choosing a project management tool based on project complexity and specific needs.

8.3 Communication and Collaboration Tools

Effective communication is essential for maintaining strong client relationships, especially for remote contractors. Communication tools streamline interactions, support real-time collaboration, and help avoid misunderstandings.

Top Communication Tools for Contractors
- **Slack**: Slack is a popular messaging platform that supports real-time chat and channels for different projects. It's ideal for ongoing communication with clients or teams.

- **Microsoft Teams**: Microsoft Teams combines chat, video calls, and file sharing, making it well-suited for contractors working with clients who use Microsoft products.

- **Zoom**: Zoom is widely used for video calls, providing screen-sharing features for presentations and collaborative sessions.

Best Practices for Communication
1. **Set Availability**: Communicate your working hours and response times to manage client expectations.

2. **Use Video Calls for Key Meetings**: Video meetings are ideal for discussing important topics or troubleshooting complex issues.

3. **Document Key Points**: Follow up on discussions with summary notes to ensure clarity and alignment with clients.

This comparison chart outlines each tool's key features, making it easy to choose the best option for your communication needs.

Tool	Features	Best For
Slack	Real-time chat, project channels	Quick updates and team collaboration
Microsoft Teams	Chat, video calls, file sharing	Full suite for team and client interaction
Zoom	Video conferencing, screen sharing	Remote presentations and client meetings

8.4 Accounting and Invoicing Tools

Accurate financial tracking is essential for IT contractors. The right accounting tools can help you manage expenses, track income, and prepare for tax filing.

Popular Accounting and Invoicing Tools
- **QuickBooks**: QuickBooks is a comprehensive accounting software with features for expense tracking, invoicing, and VAT management. It's ideal for contractors looking for a full accounting solution.

- **FreeAgent**: FreeAgent is designed for UK contractors and offers VAT and self-assessment support, invoicing, and expense tracking.

- **Xero**: Xero provides robust accounting tools with multi-currency support, making it ideal for contractors with international clients.

Best Practices for Financial Management
1. **Automate Invoicing**: Use invoicing software to set up recurring invoices and reminders, which can reduce delays.

2. **Track Expenses**: Keep records of all business-related expenses to maximise tax deductions.

3. **Set Aside Tax Funds**: Allocate a percentage of your income to cover taxes, avoiding surprises when tax payments are due.

This matrix provides a quick overview of accounting tools to help you choose the best one based on your specific financial requirements.

Tool	Features	Ideal For
QuickBooks	Full accounting, VAT support	Comprehensive financial management
FreeAgent	UK-specific features, VAT, invoicing	UK contractors needing tax support
Xero	Multi-currency, expense tracking	Contractors with international clients

8.5 Cybersecurity Tools

As an IT contractor handling sensitive data, cybersecurity is essential. Protecting client information and ensuring compliance with data protection laws like GDPR should be a priority.

Key Cybersecurity Tools for Contractors

- **LastPass or 1Password**: Password managers that store complex passwords securely, helping contractors manage multiple accounts with unique, strong passwords.

- **NordVPN or ExpressVPN**: VPNs (Virtual Private Networks) secure your internet connection, protecting data when working from public networks.

- **Bitdefender or Norton**: Antivirus software that protects against malware, ransomware, and other cyber threats.

Best Practices for Cybersecurity

1. **Use Strong, Unique Passwords**: Secure your accounts by using unique passwords for each account, managed through a password manager.

2. **Enable Multi-Factor Authentication (MFA)**: MFA adds an extra layer of security by requiring a secondary form of verification.

3. **Regularly Update Software**: Keep all software and operating systems up to date to patch vulnerabilities.

This table provides a quick comparison of essential cybersecurity tools, allowing contractors to select the tools that best safeguard client data.

Tool	Primary Function	Ideal For
LastPass/1Password	Password management	Organising and securing passwords
NordVPN/ExpressVPN	Internet connection security	Securing data on public networks
Bitdefender/Norton	Antivirus protection	Protecting against malware and cyber threats

8.6 Specialised Tools for IT Contractors

Certain IT roles require specialised tools for coding, project tracking, or data analysis. Below are some commonly used tools based on field specialisation.

1. Development Tools
- **GitHub**: Essential for version control and code collaboration. GitHub allows developers to manage code and collaborate with other programmers.
- **Visual Studio Code**: A versatile code editor supporting multiple programming languages, ideal for contractors working across different coding projects.

2. Data Analysis Tools
- **Tableau**: Tableau is a powerful tool for data visualisation, making it easy to create interactive dashboards and share insights with clients.
- **Python/R**: These programming languages are used extensively for data analysis, statistical modelling, and machine learning projects.

3. System and Network Management Tools
- **Nagios**: Nagios is a popular tool for monitoring IT infrastructure, ideal for contractors in network and system management roles.
- **AWS and Azure**: Cloud platforms used for building, testing, and deploying applications, widely applicable in software development and cloud infrastructure.

This table helps contractors choose the right tools based on their specialisation, ensuring they have the necessary resources for efficient work.

Role	Essential Tools
Software Developer	GitHub, Visual Studio Code
Data Analyst	Tableau, Python, R
System Admin	Nagios, AWS, Azure

8.7 Checklist: Essential Tools for IT Contractors

Here's a checklist to ensure you're equipped with the most effective tools for managing your contracting business:

- **Select a Time Tracking Tool**: Track hours accurately for fair invoicing and reporting.

- **Choose a Project Management Tool**: Organise projects, track tasks, and communicate progress with clients.

- **Use an Accounting Tool**: Track income, expenses, and manage invoices for smooth financial operations.

- **Implement Cybersecurity Tools**: Use VPNs, antivirus, and password managers to protect client data.

- **Adopt Specialised Tools**: Choose software tailored to your field, whether development, data analysis, or system management.

Chapter 8 Summary

Equipping yourself with the right tools enhances efficiency, ensures compliance, and streamlines workflows. From time tracking to cybersecurity, each tool in this chapter is chosen to meet the unique needs of IT contractors. The visual aids provided offer guidance in selecting the most appropriate tools for your business, based on your specific projects, client requirements, and field specialisation.

In the next chapter, we'll explore the challenges and opportunities of contracting from outside the UK, including navigating international tax laws, managing remote projects, and building strong client relationships across borders.

Chapter 9

Contracting from Outside the UK

With the rise of remote work, contracting with UK clients from outside the country is more feasible than ever. However, international contracting comes with unique challenges, including tax compliance, managing client expectations, and navigating payment logistics. This chapter provides a roadmap for international contractors working with UK clients, covering legal requirements, tax considerations, communication strategies, and financial management. Visual aids, such as decision flowcharts and checklists, will guide you through these key aspects.

9.1 Understanding Visa and Legal Requirements

If you're working entirely remotely from outside the UK, you typically don't need a visa to work with UK clients. However, if you plan to travel to the UK for meetings or onsite work, you may need a visa.

Visa Options for Non-UK Contractors

1. **Standard Visitor Visa**: For contractors who need to visit the UK for meetings or negotiations but won't perform actual contract work onsite.

2. **Temporary Worker Visa**: Required for non-UK residents who plan to work onsite in the UK for an extended period.

3. **Skilled Worker Visa**: Suitable for contractors who are highly skilled and planning longer onsite assignments in the UK, provided the client can sponsor the visa.

This flowchart helps you determine whether you need a visa and which type to apply for if you plan to visit the UK for contracting work.

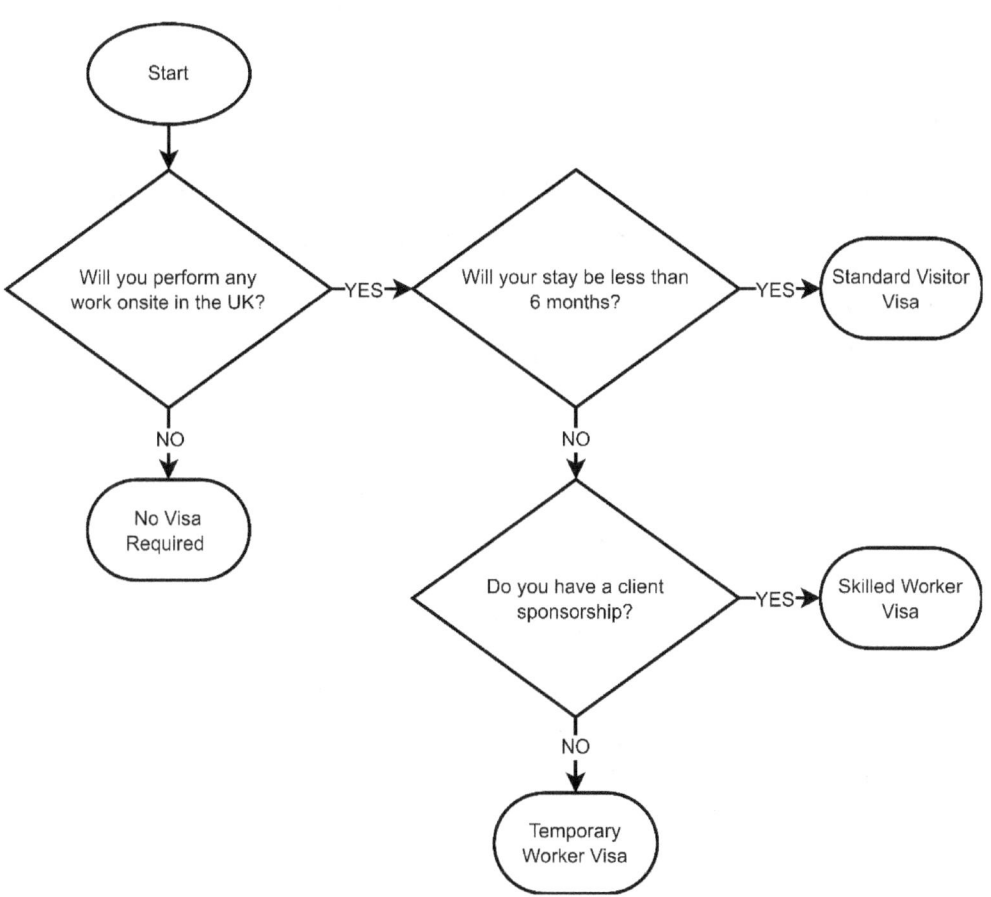

9.2 Registering Your Business for International Compliance

Operating as an international contractor requires registering your business in your home country and ensuring compliance with UK tax regulations if applicable.

Business Setup in Your Home Country

- **Sole Proprietor, LLC, or Corporation**: Choose the structure that best aligns with your country's tax advantages and requirements.
- **Multi-Currency Bank Account**: Setting up a multi-currency business account can simplify payments and help manage currency exchanges.

VAT Registration

- Contractors with UK clients may need to consider VAT registration if their turnover exceeds the UK threshold of £85,000. However, this generally only applies if you have a physical presence in the UK.
- Some contractors voluntarily register to claim VAT on expenses or use the Flat Rate VAT Scheme.

Double Taxation Treaty

- Many countries have tax treaties with the UK to avoid double taxation. Check if your country has a treaty with the UK, as this will determine which country you pay tax in on UK-based income.

The checklist below helps you navigate compliance requirements for working with UK clients as a non-UK resident.

International Compliance Checklist

1. Register Your Business Locally
   - Choose a structure that meets your tax needs
2. Set Up a Multi-Currency Business Account
   - Simplify payments and manage currency exchange
3. Check VAT Requirements
   - Determine if VAT registration is needed
4. Review Double Taxation Treaties
   - Consult tax treaties to avoid double taxation

9.3 Managing UK Taxes from Abroad

Non-UK residents may not be subject to UK taxes, but understanding UK tax requirements can ensure compliance and prevent surprises. Here's a breakdown of the primary tax considerations:

1. Understanding Your Tax Residency Status

- Non-residents typically pay taxes only in their home country, unless they have a significant UK presence or meet certain criteria.
- Consult a tax advisor to clarify your residency status, as different countries have different rules for tax residency.

2. Corporation Tax for Non-Resident Companies

- If your business operates outside the UK with no permanent establishment in the UK, it is usually exempt from UK Corporation Tax. However, any UK-based revenue may be subject to tax in your home country.

3. Personal Income Tax

- Contractors working entirely remotely may not be subject to UK income tax, but it's essential to understand any tax obligations under local tax treaties.

This flowchart helps international contractors understand their tax liabilities based on residency and double taxation agreements.

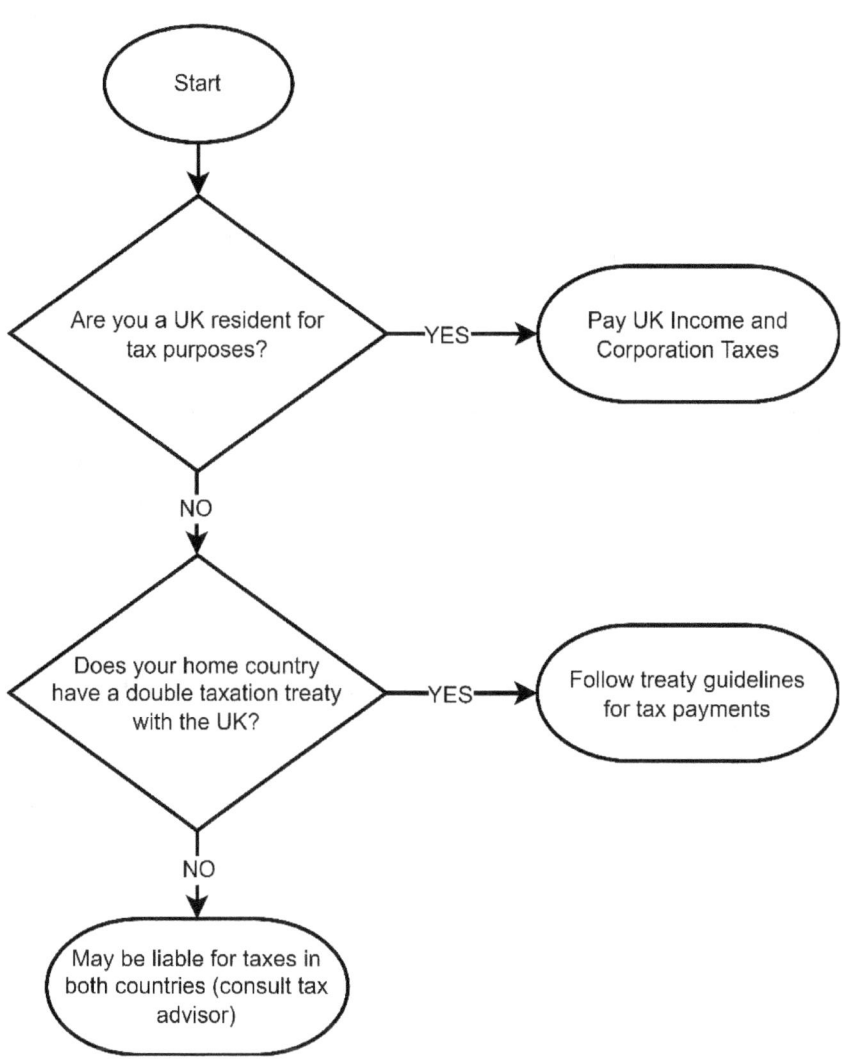

9.4 Currency Exchange and Payment Management

Currency exchange and international payment processing are important considerations for non-UK contractors. Choosing the right tools can save on fees and reduce currency exchange fluctuations.

1. Multi-Currency Bank Accounts

- **Wise (formerly TransferWise)** and **Revolut** offer multi-currency accounts, allowing you to hold GBP and convert funds when exchange rates are favourable.

2. Online Payment Platforms

- **PayPal** and **Payoneer** are widely used for international transactions. Payoneer allows direct withdrawals to local bank accounts, often at lower fees than traditional banks.

3. Minimising Exchange Fees

- To avoid frequent small exchanges, accumulate GBP earnings in a multi-currency account, then convert a larger amount when exchange rates are favourable.
- Avoid high-fee platforms like standard bank wire transfers, opting instead for services designed for international contractors.

The table above provides an overview of payment tools that facilitate efficient cross-border transactions.

Tool	Features	Best For
Wise	Multi-currency accounts, low fees	Holding and converting GBP earnings
Revolut	Real-time exchange rates, free transfers	Frequent currency conversions
Payoneer	Direct withdrawals to local accounts	Contractors preferring bank deposits
PayPal	Widely accepted, convenient	Fast, smaller transactions

9.5 Communication and Client Relationship Management

Building trust and maintaining communication with UK clients is crucial for international contractors. Time zones, language differences, and cultural nuances can affect interactions, so it's essential to implement best practices.

1. Schedule Regular Check-Ins
- Use a tool like **Calendly** or **Google Calendar** to schedule regular updates, ensuring that time zone differences are accounted for.
- Set weekly or bi-weekly meetings to discuss progress, ask questions, and address any project concerns.

2. Use Project Management Tools
- **Trello**, **Asana**, and **Jira** can help you track project progress in real time, allowing UK clients to view updates without direct communication.

3. Clarify Availability and Response Times
- Inform clients of your working hours in your time zone and establish expected response times for emails and messages.

Tool	Purpose	Best For
Calendly	Schedule meetings	Setting regular check-ins with clients
Google Calendar	Shared calendar for reminders	Coordinating across time zones
Trello/Asana	Project tracking	Real-time updates for clients
Slack	Real-time messaging	Ongoing communication and quick updates

This chart offers options for tools that simplify communication and keep international projects on track.

9.6 Client Payment Terms and Legal Protection

Securing payment and protecting your work are especially important when working across borders. Here are key strategies for payment and legal security.

1. Setting Payment Terms in Contracts

- Specify payment terms clearly, such as Net 15 or Net 30, to avoid delays.
- For larger contracts, request a deposit or use milestone-based payments to secure steady cash flow.

2. Legal Agreements

- Ensure contracts specify governing law, ideally under UK or your home country's jurisdiction, to protect yourself in case of disputes.
- Use platforms like **HelloSign** or **DocuSign** for secure contract signing and storage.

3. Payment Protection Services

- Use payment protection options on platforms like **Upwork** or **Escrow.com** for high-value projects. These options hold funds until the work is completed to both parties' satisfaction.

The checklist below helps contractors establish secure payment and legal protection practices when working internationally.

Payment and Legal Protection Checklist

1. Set Clear Payment Terms in Contracts
    - Use Net 15/30 terms and milestone payments
2. Specify Governing Law
    - Define jurisdiction to protect in case of disputes
3. Use Secure Signing Platforms
    - HelloSign or DocuSign for contract management
4. Consider Payment Protection
    - Use Upwork or Escrow.com for large projects

9.7 Checklist: Contracting from Outside the UK

This checklist covers the essential steps to manage an international contracting relationship with a UK client successfully.

- **Confirm Visa and Legal Requirements**: Determine if you need a visa for onsite work.

- **Set Up a Business Structure and Bank Account**: Register your business locally and open a multi-currency bank account.

- **Understand Tax Obligations**: Review double taxation treaties and consult a tax advisor.

- **Choose Currency and Payment Platforms**: Select a multi-currency platform for efficient payments and currency management.

- **Establish Communication Protocols**: Use scheduling and project management tools for regular updates.

- **Secure Contracts and Payment Terms**: Define payment terms, governing law, and use secure signing and payment options.

Chapter 9 Summary

Contracting from outside the UK offers flexibility and access to the UK market but requires careful planning to ensure compliance, secure payments, and effective communication. International contractors can build successful relationships with UK clients by understanding visa requirements, setting up compliant business structures, managing currency exchanges, and using the right tools for communication and legal security. The visual aids in this chapter provide an accessible guide to managing each critical aspect of international contracting.

In the final chapter, we'll discuss strategies for preparing for the future of IT contracting, including the impact of emerging trends, evolving technologies, and regulatory changes.

Chapter 10

Preparing for the Future of IT Contracting

The IT contracting landscape is continuously evolving, shaped by technological advancements, regulatory shifts, and changing client expectations. To build a sustainable contracting career, it's essential to stay adaptable, update your skills, and be aware of upcoming industry trends. In this final chapter, we'll explore future trends in IT contracting, discuss strategies for skill development, and provide practical advice on staying competitive. Visual aids, including future trend summaries, skill development guides, and a checklist for futureproofing your career, will support your journey in preparing for the future.

10.1 Future Trends in IT Contracting

Anticipating future trends in IT contracting allows you to position yourself strategically. Here are some of the key trends expected to shape the industry:

1. Increased Demand for Specialised Skills

- **Cybersecurity**: As cyber threats rise, the demand for cybersecurity expertise will continue to grow. Certifications such as CISSP, CompTIA Security+, and CISM are valuable for contractors specialising in this area.

- **AI and Machine Learning**: AI applications are expanding, and contractors with skills in machine learning, data science, and AI ethics will be in high demand.

- **Cloud Computing**: Cloud services are becoming integral to business operations, with skills in AWS, Azure, and Google Cloud positioning contractors well.

2. Growth of Remote and Hybrid Work

- Remote work continues to reshape the contracting market. Contractors who are adept at managing remote work and using collaboration tools will have a competitive advantage.

- Hybrid models are likely to increase, with contractors occasionally travelling to client locations, making flexibility essential.

3. Automation and AI in Project Management

- Many administrative tasks can now be automated, saving contractors time and allowing focus on high-impact work.
- Familiarity with automation tools like Zapier, RPA (Robotic Process Automation), and AI-driven project management platforms will be beneficial.

Trend	Impact on Contractors	Skills to Focus On
Cybersecurity Demand	High demand for data protection expertise	CISSP, CISM, CompTIA Security+
AI & ML Growth	Opportunities in data science & AI ethics	Python, Machine Learning, AI ethics
Cloud Services	More projects on cloud migration & security	AWS, Azure, Google Cloud
Remote/Hybrid Work	Flexible, remote-enabled projects increase	Remote work tools (Zoom, Slack, Asana)
Automation	Reduces time on repetitive tasks	Zapier, RPA, AI project management

This table provides a snapshot of the trends likely to shape the IT contracting landscape and the associated skills.

10.2 Adapting to Regulatory Changes

Changes in tax laws, data privacy, and compliance regulations impact how contractors operate. Staying informed helps you manage your business effectively and maintain compliance.

1. Monitoring Tax Changes

- **IR35**: Monitor updates to IR35 legislation as the UK government may continue to adjust its scope. Understanding how IR35 affects local and remote contractors is essential for tax compliance.
- **VAT and Digital Taxes**: As digital services grow, new tax regulations, such as digital service taxes, may apply to certain international contractors.

2. Staying GDPR Compliant

- Contractors working with UK or EU clients must understand GDPR and ensure they handle data appropriately. Familiarise yourself with GDPR-compliant tools and practices to protect client data and avoid penalties.

3. Consulting with Tax Advisors

- Regularly consult a tax advisor to stay current on new regulations and ensure you maximise tax efficiency within compliance.

This checklist provides key points for staying compliant with evolving regulations, particularly around IR35 and GDPR.

Regulatory Compliance Checklist

1. Monitor IR35 Changes
    - Keep up with IR35 updates affecting contractors
2. Stay GDPR Compliant
    - Use GDPR-compliant tools for client data
3. Review Digital Service Tax (if applicable)
4. Consult with Tax Advisors Annually
    - Ensure compliance and tax efficiency

10.3 Futureproofing Your Skills and Knowledge

Adapting to changes in the contracting industry requires continuous skill development. Here's how to stay competitive by building future-proof skills.

1. Upskilling in Emerging Technologies
- **AI and Data Science**: Courses on Coursera, Udacity, and LinkedIn Learning offer specialised AI and data science training.
- **Cloud Certifications**: Certifications in AWS, Azure, or Google Cloud provide contractors with a competitive edge in cloud computing roles.

2. Enhancing Project Management and Soft Skills
- **Agile and Scrum**: Agile methodologies are increasingly popular in tech projects. Consider a Scrum certification if you work in project-based roles.
- **Client Communication**: Effective communication is crucial, especially in remote and hybrid environments. Training in soft skills like negotiation, presentation, and client management can make you stand out.

3. Staying Informed Through Professional Networks
- **Join Industry Groups**: Groups like the British Computer Society (BCS), online communities, and LinkedIn groups can keep you updated on industry trends.
- **Attend Conferences**: Events like London Tech Week, Web Summit, and niche conferences are excellent for learning about innovations in your field.

This table offers a structured approach to skill development with recommended certifications and platforms.

Skill Area	Recommended Certifications/Training	Platform
Cloud Computing	AWS Solutions Architect, Microsoft Azure Certified	AWS, Microsoft, Google
Data Science & AI	Machine Learning (Coursera), Data Science (Udacity)	Coursera, Udacity, LinkedIn
Project Management	ScrumMaster, Agile Certifications	Scrum Alliance, PMI
Communication	Soft Skills, Negotiation, Client Management	LinkedIn Learning, Coursera

10.4 Leveraging Technology to Improve Efficiency

Adopting the right technology can enhance your efficiency and make managing projects and clients more seamless.

1. Automate Repetitive Tasks
- Use tools like **Zapier** to automate workflows between apps, such as automating invoice reminders or updating project management tasks.
- Implement **Robotic Process Automation (RPA)** for more complex repetitive tasks, if applicable.

2. AI-Driven Project Management Tools
- **Monday.com** and **Asana** now offer AI features for task prioritisation and deadline estimation. Using AI-driven insights can optimise project timelines and resource allocation.

3. Digital Contracts and Document Management
- Use DocuSign or HelloSign for secure, digital contract management. These platforms also store signed contracts, making it easier to manage multiple clients.

Tool	Purpose	Benefits
Zapier	Workflow automation	Saves time on repetitive tasks
Monday.com AI	Project management with AI insights	Optimises task scheduling and deadlines
DocuSign	Digital contract signing	Secure and efficient document handling
RPA Tools	Automate complex workflows	Reduces manual input for high-volume tasks

This table highlights efficiency tools that can reduce workload and improve productivity.

10.5 Expanding Your Client Base Internationally

As remote work grows, international opportunities are increasing. Expanding your client base globally can provide greater job security and open up new career paths.

1. Leverage Online Platforms for International Clients

- Platforms like **Upwork**, **Toptal**, and **Freelancer.com** allow you to connect with clients worldwide. Tailor your profile to showcase international experience and adaptability.

2. Develop a Strong Online Presence

- A professional website and active LinkedIn profile help you build credibility and attract international clients. Share testimonials from previous clients to establish trust and authority.

3. Understand Cross-Border Tax Requirements

- Expanding internationally requires understanding tax obligations across different countries. Consult a tax advisor with international experience to ensure compliance and avoid double taxation.

This checklist helps contractors navigate the steps to expand their client base across borders.

Steps to Expand Client Base Internationally
1. Register on Global Platforms   - Upwork, Toptal
2. Build a Professional Online Presence   - Website and LinkedIn profile
3. Leverage International Testimonials
4. Consult International Tax Advisors   - Ensure compliance with cross-border regulations

10.6 Checklist: Futureproofing Your IT Contracting Career

This checklist summarises actions you can take to prepare for future trends and remain competitive in the evolving IT contracting industry.

- **Stay Updated on Industry Trends**: Follow tech news, attend webinars, and join industry associations to stay ahead.

- **Invest in In-Demand Skills**: Pursue certifications and courses in AI, cloud computing, cybersecurity, and project management.

- **Use Technology to Automate Tasks**: Implement tools for workflow automation, project management, and client communication.

- **Expand Your Client Base Globally**: Leverage online platforms, build a strong online presence, and seek international opportunities.

- **Maintain Compliance**: Regularly consult tax and legal advisors to stay compliant with evolving regulations, particularly for IR35 and international taxes.

Chapter 10 Summary

Preparing for the future of IT contracting involves anticipating industry trends, building versatile skills, and using technology to increase efficiency. Focusing on high-demand areas like cybersecurity, cloud computing, and AI can help you stay competitive in a shifting market. Expanding your client base internationally and staying compliant with regulatory changes further strengthens your resilience as a contractor. This chapter's visual aids offer clear strategies for adapting to changes and futureproofing your career in IT contracting.

Thank you for reading *IT Contracting – Unlocked*. With the insights and resources provided in this book, you're well-prepared to navigate the complexities of IT contracting and achieve lasting success in this dynamic industry.

Conclusion

IT Contracting – Unlocked has guided you through every aspect of a successful IT contracting career, from selecting a business structure and navigating tax requirements to managing client relationships and preparing for future industry changes. Contracting offers flexibility, higher earning potential, and diverse opportunities, but it also demands strategic planning, strong financial management, and continuous skill development.

This conclusion summarises the core concepts covered in the book and includes visual aids that highlight essential takeaways and action items to support your journey as a successful IT contractor.

Key Takeaways

1. Setting Up for Success
- **Choose the Right Business Structure**: Selecting between a limited company, umbrella company, or sole trader model has lasting impacts on tax obligations, income structure, and administrative responsibilities.

- **Understand Tax and Compliance**: Navigating IR35, VAT, and other tax regulations is essential for protecting your income and ensuring compliance with UK laws.

2. Building Strong Client Relationships
- **Clear Contracts and Expectations**: A well-defined contract sets the foundation for a successful project. Establishing expectations on deliverables, deadlines, and payment terms promotes transparency and trust.

- **Effective Communication**: Regular updates, clear availability, and responsiveness make a positive impression and help manage client expectations effectively.

3. Financial and Legal Management
- **Track Finances and Plan for Taxes**: Using accounting tools and setting aside funds for taxes ensures smooth financial management and avoids year-end surprises.

- **Secure Contracts and Payments**: Using digital contract tools and establishing secure payment terms protects your business and income.

4. Futureproofing Your Career

- **Stay ahead of Industry Trends**: Investing in emerging skills—such as AI, cloud computing, and cybersecurity—will keep you relevant in an evolving market.

- **Leverage Technology**: Automating workflows and using project management tools increase productivity and allow you to focus on high-value tasks.

- **Expand Your Network**: Engaging with industry groups and exploring international opportunities strengthens your client base and supports a sustainable career.

Aspect	Action Item	Benefit
Business Structure	Choose between limited, umbrella, sole trader	Impacts tax, income, and admin workload
Client Management	Set clear expectations and maintain communication	Builds trust, improves satisfaction
Financial Management	Track income, set aside tax funds	Ensures financial stability and compliance
Future Skill Development	Focus on AI, cloud, cybersecurity	Prepares for changing market demands
Technology Use	Use automation and project tools	Increases productivity

This summary table distils the core action items into practical steps for maximising success in IT contracting.

Actionable Checklist for Success in IT Contracting

As a final reference, here's a checklist to help you implement the strategies covered throughout this book.

1. **Select and Register Your Business Structure**
   - Determine the best structure (limited, umbrella, sole trader) and register with the appropriate authorities.

2. **Understand and Comply with IR35**
   - Assess each contract's IR35 status, especially if you plan to work through a limited company.

3. **Use Essential Tools**
   - Invest in tools for time tracking, project management, communication, and financial management.

4. **Build and Maintain Client Relationships**
   - Set clear project expectations, communicate regularly, and request feedback to improve your services.

5. **Invest in Skill Development**
   - Pursue certifications and courses in high-demand areas like AI, cloud, and cybersecurity to stay competitive.

6. **Plan for the Future**
   - Stay informed on industry trends, leverage new technology, and expand your client base internationally when possible.

Actionable Checklist for Success in IT Contracting

This checklist provides a consolidated view of actions that will set you up for success and growth in the IT contracting world.

Success Checklist for IT Contractors
1. Select and Register Your Business Structure
2. Comply with IR35 and Tax Regulations
3. Use Essential Tools for Productivity
4. Build Strong Client Relationships
5. Invest in Continuous Skill Development
6. Plan for the Future and Adapt to Trends

Final Thoughts

The IT contracting industry offers diverse, rewarding opportunities for those who approach it with preparation and foresight. By following the strategies outlined in this book, you can build a sustainable contracting business that adapts to industry changes, leverages emerging technologies and meets evolving client needs. As you implement these insights, remember that the keys to a successful contracting career are flexibility, proactive skill development, and a commitment to high-quality client service.

Thank you for taking the time to explore *IT Contracting – Unlocked*. Equipped with the knowledge and tools provided here, you're well-prepared to navigate the complexities of IT contracting and make the most of the opportunities it offers. Here's to your success in building a fulfilling, future-ready IT

Appendices

These appendices provide additional resources, templates, and references to support you as you establish and grow your IT contracting career. These resources include a sample contract template, a glossary of key terms, a list of essential websites and tools, and professional organisations that can offer further support. Use these appendices as a quick reference guide throughout your contracting journey.

Appendix A: Sample Contract Template

Having a clear, comprehensive contract is essential for protecting both you and your client. Here's a sample contract outline that you can customise to suit specific projects and legal requirements.

Sample IT Contractor Agreement

This Contract Agreement ("Agreement") is made and entered into as of [Date] by and between [Client's Company Name], with its principal office at [Client's Address] ("Client") and [Your Company Name], with its principal office at [Your Address] ("Contractor").

- Scope of Work (SOW)
- Detailed list of services and deliverables.
- Clear outline of project milestones, timelines, and specific outcomes.

Payment Terms
- Rate structure (hourly, daily, or per project).
- Invoicing frequency (e.g., monthly) and payment terms (e.g., Net 30 days).

Intellectual Property and Confidentiality
- Ownership of work created, transfer of IP rights, and confidentiality requirements.

Termination Clause
- Conditions and notice period for early termination by either party.

Governing Law
- Specify legal jurisdiction (e.g., UK law) to resolve potential disputes.

Appendix B: Glossary of Key Terms

Understanding industry-specific terminology is essential for communicating effectively with clients and agencies. Here are some key terms every IT contractor should know:

- **Contractor**: An independent professional providing services on a project basis, typically for multiple clients.

- **Scope of Work (SOW)**: A section in the contract that defines the project's goals, deliverables, and tasks.

- **IR35**: UK tax legislation that determines if a contractor is a genuine self-employed individual or a "disguised employee."

- **PAYE (Pay As You Earn)**: A UK tax system for deducting income tax and National Insurance from employees' earnings.

- **GDPR (General Data Protection Regulation)**: EU legislation regulating data protection and privacy, applicable to contractors handling EU/UK client data.

- **VAT (Value Added Tax)**: A tax on goods and services, applicable to contractors with UK clients if turnover exceeds the VAT threshold.

This quick-reference table clarifies common industry terms, supporting clear communication with clients and agencies.

Term	Definition
Contractor	Independent worker hired for specific projects
Scope of Work (SOW)	Defines project tasks, deliverables, and timelines
IR35	Determines contractor tax status in the UK
PAYE	Tax on employee income, deducted at source
GDPR	EU data privacy legislation
VAT	Tax on goods/services over a specified income level

Appendix C: Essential Websites and Online Resources

Job Boards and Freelance Platforms

- **CWJobs**: IT-focused job board for UK contract roles – www.cwjobs.co.uk

- **LinkedIn Jobs**: Networking and job search platform with extensive contract listings – www.linkedin.com/jobs

- **Upwork**: Global freelance platform for remote contract work – www.upwork.com

Tax and Compliance Resources

- **HMRC**: UK tax authority, providing resources on IR35, VAT, and self-assessment – www.gov.uk/hmrc

- **CEST Tool**: HMRC's Check Employment Status for Tax tool, which helps determine IR35 status – www.gov.uk/guidance/check-employment-status-for-tax

Professional Networking and Industry Groups

- **Contractor UK**: A forum and resource site offering news and advice for UK contractors – www.contractoruk.com

- **British Computer Society (BCS)**: Professional association for IT professionals – www.bcs.org

This table categorises websites into job boards, tax resources, and professional groups for quick access.

Essential Online Resources
Job Boards   - CWJobs   - LinkedIn Jobs
Tax and Compliance   - HMRC   - CEST Tool
Professional Networking   - Contractor UK   - British Computer Society (BCS)

Appendix D: Recommended Tools for IT Contractors

1. Time Tracking and Invoicing Tools

- **Toggl**: Simple, intuitive time tracking tool for hourly or project-based work.
- **Harvest**: Time tracking with built-in invoicing, ideal for managing multiple clients.
- **QuickBooks**: Accounting software with VAT, invoicing, and expense tracking capabilities.

2. Project Management Tools

- **Trello**: Visual board-based tool to manage tasks and track progress.
- **Asana**: Task and project management with timelines and calendar views.
- **Jira**: Agile-friendly project management platform for software development.

3. Cybersecurity Tools

- **LastPass**: Password manager for secure login storage.
- **NordVPN**: VPN service to protect your internet connection and ensure data security.
- **Bitdefender**: Antivirus software for comprehensive protection.

This matrix helps you quickly identify essential tools across various categories, making it easy to build a complete toolkit for your contracting needs.

Tool	Category	Best For
Toggl	Time Tracking	Simple time logging across projects
QuickBooks	Accounting & Invoicing	Managing invoices and VAT
Trello	Project Management	Visual task tracking and team collaboration
LastPass	Cybersecurity	Password management
NordVPN	Cybersecurity	Protecting online activity on public networks

Appendix E: Professional Organisations and Industry Events

Staying connected with industry organisations and attending events can help you stay current with industry trends, build your network, and find new opportunities.

1. Professional Organisations

- **British Computer Society (BCS)**: Provides resources, certifications, and networking opportunities for IT professionals.
- **TechUK**: Association for the UK technology sector, offering insights on industry trends and policy.

2. Industry Events

- **London Tech Week**: One of the UK's largest technology events, covering a wide range of IT topics.
- **Cyber Security & Cloud Expo**: Focuses on cybersecurity and cloud innovations, essential for contractors specialising in these areas.
- **Web Summit**: Global technology conference with speakers and networking opportunities.

This table categorises organisations and events, helping you identify those most relevant to your contracting career and specialisation.

Organisation/Event	Focus Area	Benefits
British Computer Society (BCS)	IT professional development	Certifications, networking, industry updates
TechUK	UK tech sector	Industry trends, policy updates
London Tech Week	Technology innovation	Networking, trends, and educational sessions
Cyber Security & Cloud Expo	Cybersecurity and cloud tech	Specialised insights for security contractors
Web Summit	Global tech trends	Exposure to global innovations

Appendix F: Checklist for Contracting Success

Use this checklist to ensure you're equipped with the resources and strategies necessary for a successful IT contracting career.

- **Set Up Business Structure and Compliance**: Register your business and ensure VAT and IR35 compliance.

- **Create a Professional Contract Template**: Develop a contract template that covers essential elements like scope, payment, and IP.

- **Invest in Essential Tools**: Based on your specific needs, select tools for time tracking, project management, and cybersecurity.

- **Engage with Professional Organisations**: Join relevant organisations and attend industry events to expand your network and stay updated.

- **Stay Informed on Industry Trends**: To remain competitive and keep up with developments in AI, cybersecurity, cloud computing, and remote work.

This checklist offers a high-level overview of the steps necessary for building and sustaining a successful contracting career.

Contracting Success Checklist
1. Set Up Business Structure and Compliance
2. Develop a Contract Template
3. Invest in Essential Tool
4. Join Professional Organisations
5. Stay Informed on Industry Trends

These appendices provide practical resources, insights, and references to help you navigate the world of IT contracting. With templates, tools, and a clear checklist, you are equipped to handle the challenges and seize the opportunities of this dynamic field. Good luck, and here's to your continued success as an IT contractor!

About The Author

Ravi Matharu brings over 26 years of experience in the IT industry, with more than 15 years spent as an IT contractor. He began his career as a Support Analyst, and after moving into management, Ravi realised his passion lay in a technical career path. This realisation led him to the world of IT contracting, where he has thrived as a Consultant and Technical Architect, working with multiple companies and delivering value across diverse projects.

Ravi holds a wealth of certifications, including Citrix CNAs, Microsoft/Azure MCITP & MCSE, VMware VCPs, and is TOGAF 9.1 Certified. He is a firm believer in continual professional development and is currently pursuing his AWS Solutions Architect Professional certification to expand his expertise in cloud computing.

While Ravi values his certifications, he firmly believes that experience is what truly shapes an IT professional. His extensive time in the field, combined with his ongoing pursuit of knowledge, positions him as a trusted guide for those navigating the complex and rewarding world of IT contracting. Through IT Contracting Unlocked, Ravi shares his knowledge and insights to help others build successful, sustainable careers in IT contracting.

www.ingramcontent.com/pod-product-compliance
Lightning Source LLC
Chambersburg PA
CBHW071407210526
45465CB00001B/297